The Concise
PRINCE2®

Principles and essential themes

Third edition

The Concise PRINCE2®

Principles and essential themes

Third edition

COLIN BENTLEY

IT Governance Publishing

Every possible effort has been made to ensure that the information contained in this book is accurate at the time of going to press, and the publisher and the author cannot accept responsibility for any errors or omissions, however caused. Any opinions expressed in this book are those of the author, not the publisher. Websites identified are for reference only, not endorsement, and any website visits are at the reader's own risk. No responsibility for loss or damage occasioned to any person acting, or refraining from action, as a result of the material in this publication can be accepted by the publisher or the author.

PRINCE2® is a registered trade mark of AXELOS Limited. All rights reserved.

Apart from any fair dealing for the purposes of research or private study, or criticism or review, as permitted under the Copyright, Designs and Patents Act 1988, this publication may only be reproduced, stored or transmitted, in any form, or by any means, with the prior permission in writing of the publisher or, in the case of reprographic reproduction, in accordance with the terms of licences issued by the Copyright Licensing Agency. Enquiries concerning reproduction outside those terms should be sent to the publisher at the following address:

IT Governance Publishing Ltd
Unit 3, Clive Court
Bartholomew's Walk
Cambridgeshire Business Park
Ely, Cambridgeshire
CB7 4EA
United Kingdom

www.itgovernancepublishing.co.uk

First published in the United Kingdom in 2012 by IT Governance Publishing
ISBN 978-1-84928-347-2

Second edition published in the United Kingdom in 2013 by IT Governance Publishing

ISBN 978-1-84928-478-3

Third edition published in the United Kingdom in 2019 by IT Governance Publishing

ISBN 978-1-78778-060-6

ABOUT THE AUTHOR

Colin Bentley has been a project manager since 1966 and has managed many projects, large and small, in several countries. He has been working with PRINCE2®, PRINCE and its predecessor, PROMPT II, since 1975. He was one of the team that brought PROMPT II to the marketplace, wrote the original PRINCE2 manual and is the author of all revisions to the manual until the 2009 version.

He was the Chief Examiner for PRINCE2 from its beginning until 2008 and wrote all Foundation and Practitioner exam papers, and marked them until they reached the massive volumes that are sat today.

Now retired, he has had over 20 books published, has lectured widely on PRINCE2 and has acted as project management consultant to such firms as The London Stock Exchange, Microsoft Europe, Tesco Stores, Commercial Union and the BBC. He still writes books on the PRINCE2 method and has updated them all to reflect the 2017 version.

CONTENTS

Contents

INTRODUCTION

Overview

What is a project?

A project is a temporary organisation for the purpose of delivering one or more business products according to an agreed business case.

What makes projects different?

- Temporary
- Cross-functional team
- More risky than business as usual (BAU)
- Bring about change
- Unique

Project variables to be controlled:

- Costs
- Timescales
- Quality
- Scope
- Risk
- Benefits

PRINCE2® benefits:

- Any type of project
- Projects driven by viability of business case

- Recognition of responsibilities
- Product focus
- Different plan levels for different management levels
- Tolerance setting / management by exception
- Stakeholder involvement throughout the project life
- All projects share common vocabulary
- Consistency of project management
- Established and proven method
- Supports project management learning and continual improvement
- Provides assurance, assessment and audit capabilities
- Wide expertise support
- Exam-based accreditation

Principles:

- Continued business justification
- Learn from experience
- Defined roles and responsibilities
- Manage by stages
- Manage by exception
- Focus on products
- Tailor to suit the project environment

PRINCE2 structure

PRINCE2 is based on seven themes:

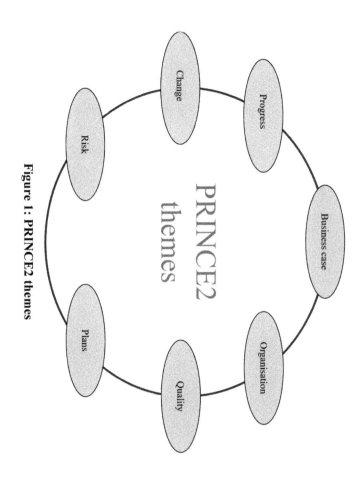

Figure 1: PRINCE2 themes

PRINCE2 consists of seven processes that cover the project lifecycle:

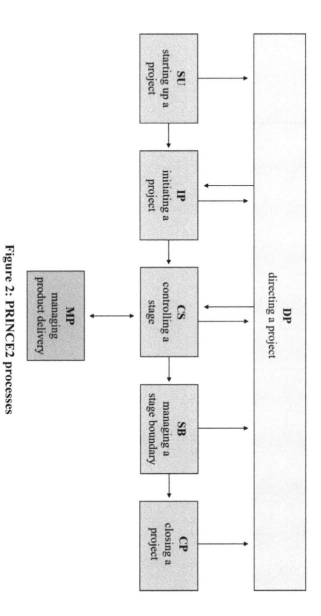

Figure 2: PRINCE2 processes

CHAPTER 1: PROCESSES

Starting up a project

Purpose

- To answer the question, 'Do we have a viable and worthwhile project?'
- To ensure prerequisites for DP (directing a project) and authorisation of IP (initiating a project) are in place.

Table 1: Starting Up a Project

Input	From	Activity	By	Output
Project mandate	Corporate or programme management	**Appoint the executive and project manager**	Corporate or programme management	Executive and project manager job descriptions
			Project manager	Daily log
Project mandate	Corporate or programme management	**Prepare the outline business case**	Executive	Outline business case
Previous lesson reports	Quality assurance	**Capture previous lessons**	Project manager	Lessons log
Executive appointment	Corporate or programme management	**Design and appoint the project management team**	• Project manager → produce • Executive → approve	Project management team structure and job descriptions

Input	From	Activity	By	Output
Project mandate	Corporate or programme management	**Select the project approach and assemble the project brief**	Project manager	• Project approach • Project brief
Project brief		**Plan the initiation stage**	Project manager	Initiation stage plan
			Project manager	Request to initiate a project

Directing a project

Purpose

- To enable the project board to be accountable for the project's success by making key decisions and exercising overall control.

Table 2: Directing a Project

Input	From	Activity	By	Output
Request to initiate a project	Project manager (SU)	**Authorise initiation**	Project board	Initiation notification
Project brief	Project manager (SU)			
Project product description	Project manager (SU)			
Project management team appointments	Project manager (SU)			
Initiation stage plan	Project manager (SU)		Project board	Authority to initiate a project
Request to deliver a project	Project manager (IP)	**Authorise the project**	Project board	Stage authorisation
Project initiation documentation	Project manager (IP)		Project board	Project authorisation notification

Input	From	Activity	By	Output
Benefits management approach	Project manager (IP)			
Request for advice	Project manager (CS)	**Give ad hoc direction**	Project board	Advice and decisions
Highlight reports	Project manager (CS)			
Exception report	Project manager (CS)		Project board	Exception plan request
Advice and decisions	Corporate / programme management		Project board	Premature close or new issue
Request to approve stage / exception plan	Project manager (SB)	**Authorise a stage or exception plan**	Project board	Stage or exception plan approval
End-stage report	Project manager (SB)			
Next stage plan or exception plan	Project manager (SB)			

Input	From	Activity	By	Output
New product descriptions	Project manager (SB)			
Project plan	Project initiation documentation			
Business case	Project initiation documentation			
Lessons report (optional)	Project manager (SB)			
End-project report	Project manager (CP)	**Authorise project closure**	Project board	
Closure recommendation	Project manager (CP)			Closure notification
Original project initiation document				

Input	From	Activity	By	Output
Lessons report	Project manager (CP)		Project board	Lessons report
Follow-on action recommendations	Project manager (CP)		Project board	Follow-on action recommendations
Benefits management approach	Project initiation document		Project board	Benefits management approach (to corporate)

Initiating a project

Purpose

- To establish solid foundations for the project; and
- To enable the project board to understand everything about the project – cost, time, benefits and risks – before committing to major expenditure.

Table 3: Initiating a Project

Input	From	Activity	By	Output
Authority to initiate the project	Project board (DP)	**Prepare the tailoring approach**	Project manager	Part of project initiation documentation
• Project brief • Daily log • Lessons log	Project manager (SU)	**Prepare the risk management approach**	Project manager	Risk management approach
			Project support	Risk register
• Project brief • Daily log • Lessons log	Project manager (SU)	**Prepare the change control approach**	Project manager	• Change control approach • Updated Project Management Team (PMT) structure • Updated job descriptions
			Project support	• Configuration item records • Issue register

Input	From	Activity	By	Output
• Business strategies • Project product description • Project brief • Daily log • Lessons log	Project manager	**Prepare the quality management approach**	Project manager	Quality management approach
			Project support	Quality register
• Business strategies • Project product description • Project brief		**Prepare the communication management approach**	Project manager	Communication management approach
• Business strategies • Project product description • Project brief • Daily log • Lessons log		**Create the project plan**	Project manager	• Project plan • Updated PMT structure • Updated job descriptions
			Project support	Configuration item records

Input	From	Activity	By	Output
Project plan	Project manager (IP)	**Set up the project controls**	Project manager	• Project controls (part of project initiation documentation) • Updated PMT structure • Updated job descriptions
Outline business case	Executive (SU)	**Refine the business case**	Project manager	Detailed business case
• Project plan • Detailed business case	Project manager (IP)		Project manager	• Benefits management approach • Updated risk register
• Business strategies • Project brief • Project plan		**Assemble the project initiation documentation**	Project manager	Project initiation documentation
				Request to deliver a project
				Stage boundary approaching

Controlling a stage

Purpose

- To assign and monitor work, deal with issues and risks, report progress and take action to ensure that the stage stays within its tolerances.

Table 4: Controlling a Stage

Input	From	Activity	By	Output
Stage authorisation	Project board (DP)	**Authorise a work package**	Project manager	Work package
Stage plan	Project manager (SB)		Project support	Updated configuration item records
Product descriptions	Project manager (SB)		Project support	Updated quality register
Team plan(s)	Team manager (MP)		Project manager	Updated risk register
Project initiation document	Project manager (IP)		Project manager	Updated issue register
(Corrective action)	Project manager (CS)			

Input	From	Activity	By	Output
Stage plan		**Review work package status**	Project manager	Updated stage plan
Work package	Team manager		Project support	Updated configuration item records
Checkpoint report	Team manager		Project manager	Updated risk register
Quality register	Project support		Project manager	Updated issue register
Team plan(s)	Team manager(s)		Project manager	Updated work package
Risk register	Project manager			
Stage plan		**Receive completed work packages**	Project manager	Updated stage plan
Configuration item records	Project support		Project support	Updated configuration item records

Input	From	Activity	By	Output
Quality register	Project support			
Stage plan	Project manager	**Review the stage status**	Project manager	Updated stage plan
Quality register	Project support		Project manager	Updated lessons log
Product status account	Project support			
Checkpoint report(s)	Team manager		Project manager	Issue report (optional)
Issue register	Project manager		Project manager	Updated issue register
Risk register	Project manager		Project manager	Updated risk register
Business case	Project initiation document			
Project plan	Project initiation document			

Input	From	Activity	By	Output
Benefits management approach	Project initiation document			
Stage plan		**Report highlights**	Project manager	Highlights report
Checkpoint reports	Team manager(s)			
Daily log	Project manager			
Lessons log	Project manager			
Quality register	Project support			
Risk register	Project manager			
Issue register	Project manager			
Product status account	Project support			
Previous highlight reports				

Input	From	Activity	By	Output
Communication management approach	Project initiation document			
New issues		**Capture and examine issues and risks**	Project manager	Updated issue register
New risks			Project manager	Issue report
Stage plan			Project manager	Updated risk register
Business case	Project initiation document		Project manager	Request for advice
Project plan	Project initiation document			
Communication management approach	Project initiation document			
Configuration management approach	Project initiation document			

1: Processes

Input	From	Activity	By	Output
Issue report		**Escalate issues and risks**	Project manager	Exception report
Issue register	Project manager		Project manager	Updated issue register
Risk register	Project manager		Project manager	Updated risk register
Business case	Project initiation document		Project manager	Updated issue report
Project plan	Project initiation document			
Daily log	Project manager	**Take corrective action**	Project manager	Updated daily log
Issue register	Project manager		Project manager	Updated issue register
Risk register	Project manager		Project manager	Updated risk register
Issue report			Project manager	Updated issue report

Input	From	Activity	By	Output
Stage plan			Project manager	Updated stage plan
Configuration item records	Project support		Project support	Updated configuration item records

Managing product delivery

Purpose

- To act as a link between the team manager and the project manager; and
- To cover the requirements for accepting, executing and delivering project work.

Table 5: Managing Product Delivery

Input	From	Activity	By	Output
Work package	Project manager (CS)	**Accept a work package**	Team manager	Team plan
			Project support	Updated quality register
			Team manager	New risk (optional)
Work package	Project manager (CS)	**Execute a work package**	Team manager	Specialist products
Team plan	Team manager		Project support	Updated quality register
			Project support	Updated configuration item records
			Team manager	Updated team plan

Input	From	Activity	By	Output
			Team manager	Checkpoint report(s)
			Team manager	Approval records
			Team manager	New risk
			Team manager	New issue
Work package	Project manager (CS)	**Deliver a work package**	Team manager	Updated work package
Quality register	Project support		Team manager	Updated team plan
Configuration item records	Project support			

Managing a stage boundary

Purpose

- To provide the project board with enough information to confirm continued viability and acceptability of risks.

Table 6: Managing a Stage Boundary

Input	From	Activity	By	Output
Stage boundary approaching	Project manager (CS)	Plan the next stage		
Current stage plan	Project manager (CS)		Project manager	Next stage plan
Project plan	Project initiation document		Project manager	Updated project plan
Issue register	Project manager		Project manager	Updated issue register
Risk register	Project manager		Project manager	Updated risk register
Project product description	Project initiation document		Project support	Configuration item record(s)
Project approach	Project initiation document		Project manager	Any revisions to project approach

Input	From	Activity	By	Output
Approaches	Project initiation document		Project manager	Any new product description(s)
			Project support	Updated quality register
Project management team	Project initiation document		Project manager	Updated PMT
Exception plan request	Project board	**Produce an exception plan**		
Exception report	Project manager (CS)			
Current stage plan	Project manager (CS)		Project manager	Exception plan
Project plan	Project initiation document		Project manager	Updated project plan
Issue register	Project manager		Project manager	Updated issue register

Input	From	Activity	By	Output
Risk register	Project manager		Project manager	Updated risk register
Project product description	Project initiation document		Project support	Configuration item record(s)
Project approach	Project initiation document		Project manager	Any revisions to project approach
Approaches	Project initiation document		Project manager	Any new product description(s)
			Project support	Updated quality register
Project plan	Project initiation document	**Update the project plan**	Project manager	Updated project plan
Current stage plan	Project manager (CS)			
Next stage plan	Project manager (SB)			

Input	From	Activity	By	Output
Project approach	Project initiation document		Project manager	Any revisions to project approach
Issue register			Project manager	Updated issue register
Risk register			Project manager	Updated risk register
Business case	Project initiation document	**Update the business case**	Project manager	Updated business case
Benefits management approach	Project initiation document		Project manager	Updated benefits management approach
Project plan	Project initiation document			
Issue register			Project manager	Updated issue register
Risk appetite (any revision)	Corporate / programme management			
Risk register			Project manager	Updated risk register

Input	From	Activity	By	Output
Project plan	Project initiation document	**Report stage end**	Project manager	End-stage report
Current stage plan				

Closing a project

Purpose

- Obtain confirmation that the project product has been accepted; and
- Recognise that the objectives in the Project Initiation Documentation (PID) and agreed changes have been achieved (i.e. recognise that the project has nothing more to contribute).

Table 7: Closing a Project

Input	From	Activity	By	Output
Project end approaching	Project manager (CS)	**Prepare planned closure**		
Product status account	Project support			
Project plan	Project initiation document		Project manager	Updated project plan
Current stage plan	Project manager (CS)			
Project product description	Project initiation document			
Premature close instruction		**Prepare premature closure**		
Product status account	Project support			

Input	From	Activity	By	Output
Project plan	Project initiation document		Project manager	Updated project plan
Current stage plan	Project manager (CS)		Project manager	Additional work estimates
Project product description	Project initiation document			
Issue register	Project manager		Project manager	Updated issue register
Issue report (optional)	Project manager (CS)		Project manager	Updated issue report (optional)
Acceptance records	Users (project manager to obtain)	**Hand over products**	Project manager	Follow-on action recommendations
Issue register	Project manager		Project support	Updated configuration item records
Risk register	Project manager		Project manager	Benefits management approach

Input	From	Activity	By	Output
Configuration management approach	Project initiation document			
Acceptance	Operations and maintenance groups			
Project initiation document		**Evaluate the project**	Project manager	End-project report
Follow-on action recommendations			Project manager	Lessons report
Communication management approach	Project initiation document	**Recommend project closure**	Project manager	Closure recommendation
			Project manager	Closed issue register
			Project manager	Closed risk register
			Project manager	Closed quality register

Input	From	Activity	By	Output
			Project manager	Closed lessons log
			Project manager	Closed daily log
Configuration management approach	Project initiation document		Project support	Archived project records

CHAPTER 2: THEMES

Business case

Purpose

To set up mechanisms to judge whether the project is (and remains):

- Viable;
- Desirable; and
- Achievable

in order to support decisions on its (continued) investment.

Table 8: Business Case Lifecycle

Outline	SU
Develop	IP
Impact analysis of issues and risks	CS
Maintain	SB
Verify	DP
Confirm	Post-project and DP (any mid-project benefits)

Table 9: Basic Business Options

Do nothing	Do the minimum	Do something

Table 10: Business Case Responsibilities

Role	Responsibilities
Corporate / programme management	• Provide the project mandate (business reasons) • Define any standards or format for the business case • Hold the senior user role responsible for benefit measurement • Responsible for the benefit management approach post-project
Executive	• Responsible for the business case during the project • Verify claimed benefits match business strategies and are achievable • Accountable for the benefits management approach during the project unless done by corporate / programme management

	• Secure project funding and project tolerances
Senior user	• Specify the required project outcome • Estimate the project benefits • Record the pre-project situation for later benefit measurement • Monitor product development to ensure the expected benefits will be realised • Measure actual benefit achievement
Senior supplier	• Supplier business case • Confirm viability of project plan
Project manager	• Business case development • Benefits management approach • Update both of the above at each end-stage assessment • Review impact of risks and issues on business case viability

Project assurance	• Monitor the project for any business case change • Participate in reviews of potential changes for any impact on the project plan and business case
Project support	• Change control and version control of the business case and benefits management approach

Benefits of management approach

Management actions to ensure project's outcomes are achieved and confirm benefits are obtained.

Table 11: Benefits of Management Approach

Action	When	By	Description
Created	IP	PM	Submitted to PB
Approval	DP	PB	Part of project approval
Updated	CS and SB	PM	Any benefits achieved and updates to benefits

			management approach
Achieved benefit confirmation	SB	Senior user	Pass to PM for reporting in end-stage report
Planning post-project reviews	CP	Executive	Done by programme management if part of a programme
Review of benefit achievement	Post-project	Senior user	Held responsible by corporate / programme management

Summary

- No project should start without business justification;
- If the justification disappears, the project should be stopped;
- The business case drives decision-making;
- Benefits should be measurable;
- Most benefits are realised post-project; and
- Risk and change evaluation should include impact on business case.

Table 12: Special Terms

Output	Any tangible or intangible specialist product created by the project
Outcome	Result of the change derived from using the project's products
Benefit	Measurable improvement resulting from an outcome
Dis-benefit	Negative impact

Organisation

Purpose

- To establish the project's structure of accountability and responsibilities.

Summary

- PRINCE2® is based on a customer / supplier environment;
- Every project needs effective direction, management, control and communication; and
- Every project needs (decision-making) representation from stakeholders:

Table 13: Stakeholder Decision-making Representation

	Corporate / programme management	Project board
Business	Executive	
User	Senior user	
Supplier	Senior supplier	

Table 14: Four Management Levels

1. **Corporate or programme management**	Commissioning
2. **Project board**	Directing
3. **Project manager**	Managing
4. **Team manager**	Delivering

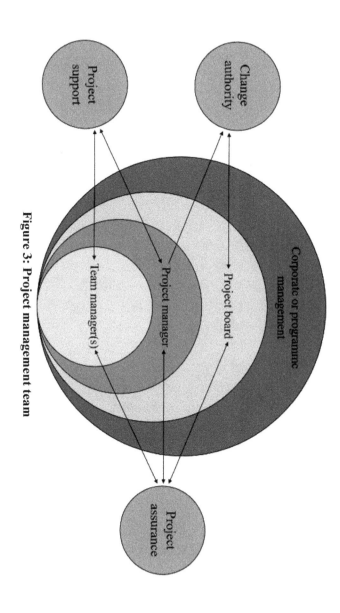

Figure 3: Project management team

- Project board = decision-making + accountability.
- Roles can be combined or shared, but not eliminated, according to the project's size and complexity.
- PRINCE2 does not recommend sharing the executive or project manager roles.
- Project board members can delegate some activities (not decisions) to project assurance.
- Project board may appoint a change authority to handle change requests.
- Project management team should be reviewed at every stage end (SB) to see if changes are needed.
- Communication needs of stakeholders defined in communication management approach.
- Communication needs of project board defined in project controls.

Related principles

- Continued business justification
- Defined roles and responsibilities
- Manage by stages
- Manage by exception
- Tailor to suit the environment

Answers

- Accountability
- Who is responsible for what?
- Who reports to whom?

Who

Table 15: Responsibilities – Organisation

Product	Responsible	When
Executive appointment	Corporate / programme	SU
Project manager appointment	Executive	SU
Project management team design	Project manager	SU
Project communication approach	Project manager	IP
Stakeholder engagement	Project manager	CS and SB
Resource commitment	Project board	DP
Project management team changes	Project manager and project board	SB

Table 16: Possible Programme Roles in a Project

Programme role	Project role
Programme manager	Executive
Business change manager	Senior user or executive
Programme design authority	Change authority or project assurance
Programme office	Project support

Special terms

- Executive
- Senior user
- Senior supplier
- Project board
- Project assurance
- Change authority

Plans

Purpose

- Define the what, how, where, when and by whom products are to be created.

Summary

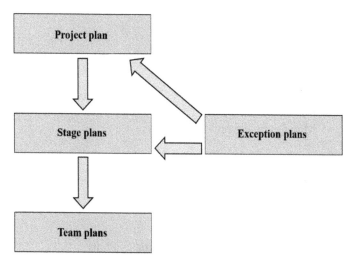

Figure 4: Levels of plan

- Provides a baseline for measuring progress
- Enables thinking ahead
- Helps avoid omissions and duplication
- Helps identify threats and opportunities
- Facilitates communication and control
- Provides a basis for control

Planning steps

Analyse the risks in each of the following steps:

- Designing the plan
- Defining and analysing the products (PBP)

- Identifying activities and dependencies
- Preparing estimates
- Preparing the schedule
- Documenting the plan

Related principles

- Focus on products
- Manage by stages

Answers

- Are the targets achievable?

Who

Table 17: Responsibilities – Plans

Product	Responsible	When
Initiation stage plan	Project manager	SU
Project plan	Project manager	IP
Stage plans	Project manager	SB
Team plans	Team manager	MP

Special terms

Product breakdown structure

A hierarchy of all the products to be produced during a plan.

Product flow diagram

A diagram of the sequence and interdependencies of producing the products of a plan.

Product description

The description of a product's purpose, content, derivation, quality criteria and any quality tolerance.

Project product description

Describes the project's end products, the customer's quality expectations, acceptance criteria and acceptance methods.

Exception plan

A plan to replace the remaining part of a plan that can no longer be achieved.

Quality

Purpose

To define and implement how the project will create and verify products that are fit for purpose.

Definition

The degree to which a set of inherent characteristics of a product, service, process, organisation, system or resource fulfils requirements.

Summary

- Aim of theme – common understanding of the criteria against which the quality of the project's products will be assessed; and
- Quality of management as well as specialist products.

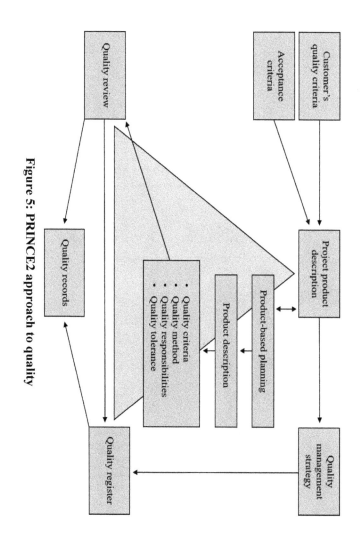

Figure 5: PRINCE2 approach to quality

Table 18: Quality Acceptance Criteria

	Acceptance criteria
MoSCoW	**M**ust have
	Should have
	Could have
	Won't have for now

Quality management approach

- How quality will be managed in the project
- Created in IP, reviewed in every SB

Quality register

- Diary of all quality events, planned and performed
- Created in IP, updated throughout (CS, MP), reviewed every SB

Quality tolerances

Examples:

- Maintain office temperature at 22 degrees C (within -1 to +3)
- Sermon should last 10 minutes (-2 to +5 minutes)

Table 19: Quality Review

Quality review	Input	Output
Preparation	Product description invitation	• Question lists • Annotated copies
Review	Product	• Follow-up action list • Updated quality register • Updated CIR
Follow-up	Follow-up action list	• Sign-off • Updated quality register • Updated configuration item record
Roles	Chair	Presenter
	Reviewer	Administrator

Related principles

• Focus on products
• Learn from experience

Answers

- Will products meet business expectations?
- Will the desired benefits be achieved subsequently?

Who

Table 20: Responsibilities – Quality

Role	Responsibilities
Corporate / programme management	• Provide corporate / programme or customer quality system
Executive	• Sign off project product description • Sign off quality management approach • Confirm product acceptance
Senior user	• Customer's quality expectations and acceptance criteria • Agree quality management approach • Approve product descriptions of user products • Provide user resources for quality checking • Sign off finished products

Senior supplier	<ul><li>Agree quality management approach</li><li>Agree quality methods, tools and techniques to be used</li><li>Approve specialist product descriptions</li></ul>
Project manager	<ul><li>Prepare project product description</li><li>Create quality management approach</li><li>Create product descriptions</li><li>Ensure work packages contain quality requirements</li></ul>
Team manager	<ul><li>Assist in writing product descriptions</li><li>Ensure quality work carried out</li><li>Ensure quality work recorded</li></ul>
Project assurance	<ul><li>Review product descriptions</li><li>Advise on suitable quality reviewers</li><li>Assure project board on implementation of quality management approach</li></ul>

Special terms

- Customer's quality expectations
- Product description
- Quality criteria
- Quality review
- Quality assurance (site-wide) independent of project

Risks

Purpose

Identify, assess and control uncertainty.

Summary

- Risk is an uncertain event or set of events that, should it occur, will have an effect on the achievement of objectives;
- Threat – negative effect; and
- Opportunity – positive effect.

Table 21: Risk Management Procedure

Risk management procedure			
1. Identify	2. Assess	3. Plan	4. Implement
5. Communicate			

Identify – cause / event / effect.

Table 22: Risk Responses

Threat	Opportunity
Avoid	Exploit
Reduce	Enhance
Transfer	Reject
Share	Share
Accept	

Prepare contingency plans	

Related principles

- Continued business justification

Answers

- Probability – how likely
- Impact – how much
- Proximity – how soon

Who

Table 23: Responsibilities – Risk

Product	Responsible	When
Risk appetite	Corporate / programme	SU
Risk management approach	Project manager	IP
Risk register	Project support	IP

Risk management approach

- How will risks be controlled (responsibilities, processes, procedures, techniques, documents).

Special terms

Table 24: Special Terms

Risk appetite	Amount of risk an organisation considers acceptable.
Risk tolerance	Risk threshold that when threatened will trigger an exception report.
Risk owner	Responsible for the management, monitoring and control of an assigned risk.
Risk actionee	Assigned to carry out a risk response action.
Risk profile	Probability / impact grid showing risk tolerances boundary.
Risk budget	Sum of money set aside for fallback plans.

Risk responsibilities

Table 25: Responsibilities – Risk

Role	Responsibilities
Corporate / programme management or customer	Risk management policy
Executive	• Check risk management approach is suitable • Business case risk identification
Senior user	User risk identification (on benefits, operational use, maintenance)
Senior supplier	Product development risks
Project manager	• Risk management approach • Risk register • Execution of risk management approach
Team manager	Risk identification and control in work packages

| Project assurance | Monitor use of the approach |

Change

Purpose

Identify, assess and control potential and approved changes to the baseline.

Baseline

A 'frozen' or fixed version of a product, used as a reference point, e.g. for future work based on it or a product ready for quality review.

Summary

Covers issue / change control.

Table 26: Issue and Change Control Procedure

Issue and change control procedure				
Capture	Examine	Propose	Decide	Implement

Table 27: Types of Issue

Types of issue		
Request for change (RFC)	Off-specification (O-S)	Problem / concern

Related principles

- Continued business justification
- Manage by exception
- Defined roles and responsibilities

Answers

- What does anyone want to change, delete or add after the project initiation documentation is agreed?
- What would be the impact of a change?
- Product status

Who

Table 28: Responsibilities – Change

Product	Responsible	When
Configuration item record(s)	Project manager	SB
Daily log	Project manager	SU
Issue register	Project support	IP
Issue report	Project manager	CS
Product status account	Project support	CS / SB

Special terms

Table 29: Special Terms

Change authority	Project board delegates some decisions on changes within limits
Change budget	• Funds changes and analysis costs • Linked to change authority
Concession	Acceptance by the project board of a product that fails to fully meet its specification

Progress

Purpose

Establish mechanisms to:

- Compare actual progress against planned;
- Forecast project completion;
- Review continued viability; and
- Control unacceptable deviations.

Summary

Progress controls ensure that for each level of the project management team, the next higher level can:

- Monitor progress;
- Compare level of achievement with plan;
- Review plans and options against future situations;

- Detect problems and identify risks; and
- Authorise future work.

Table 30: Progress Controls

In	Out
Corporate / programme management	
• Overall requirements • Project tolerances	Project progress / exceptions
Project board	
• Stage authorisations • Stage tolerances	• Project initiation document • New stage plans • Highlights reports • End-stage reports • Exception reports • End-project report
Project manager	
Work package and tolerances	Checkpoint reports
Team manager	

Tolerances define the amount of discretion that each management level can exercise without the need to refer up to the next level for approval.

Table 31: Tolerances

Area	Project level	Stage level	Work package level	Product
Time	Project plan	Stage plan	Work package	
Cost	Project plan	Stage plan	Work package	
Scope	Project plan	Stage plan	Work package	
Risk	Risk management approach	Stage plan	Work package	
Quality	Project product description			Product description

Benefits	Business case			

An exception is a situation where it can be forecast that there will be a deviation beyond the agreed tolerance levels.

Management stages

- Partitions of the project with management decision points
- Collection of activities and products whose delivery is managed as a unit
- The element of work delegated by the project board to the project manager at any one time

Table 32: Management Stage Benefits

Management stage benefits
Gives the project board the opportunity to assess project viability at key moments.
Allows key decisions to be made before the detailed work needed to implement them.
Facilitates management by exception by authorising only one stage at a time.

Business case and project plan reviewed before committing to a stage.
Project manager can make adjustments as long as within stage tolerances.

Number of stages criteria:

- Must be at least two (initiation and the rest of the project)
- How far ahead is it sensible to plan?
- When are the key decision points?
- How risky is the project? (more risks = shorter stages)
- Too many short stages increase management overhead
- Too few long stages reduce project board control
- Project board and project manager confidence levels

Event-driven controls:

- End-stage reports
- End-project report
- Exception report
- Project initiation document completion

Time-driven controls:

- Checkpoint reports
- Highlights report

Related principles

- Manage by exception
- Continued business justification
- Manage by stages

Answers

- Where are we now?
- How does this compare with where we planned to be?
- Is the project still viable?
- Are we still confident about the way forward?

Who

Table 33: Responsibilities – Progress

Product	Responsible	When
Checkpoint report	Team manager	Frequency agreed in work package
Highlights report	Project manager	Frequency agreed with project board
End-stage report	Project manager	End of stage

Exception report	Project manager	Forecast tolerance exception
End-project report	Project manager	Close of project

Special terms

Table 34: Special Terms

Tolerance	Permissible deviation above and below a planned target
Exception	A forecast deviation beyond the agreed tolerance

CHAPTER 3: TECHNIQUES

Product-based planning

PRINCE2® planning philosophy is to first identify the required products, then the activities, dependencies and resources required to deliver the products.

There are four tasks in product-based planning:

Table 35: Product-based Planning Tasks

Task	When	Description
1. Write the project product description	Once as part of starting up a project	This is a specialised form of product description, defining the scope, requirements, customer's quality expectations and acceptance criteria.
2. Create the product breakdown structure	For all levels of plan	Break the plan down into the major products to be delivered. Further break these down until an appropriate

		level of detail for the plan is reached.
3. Write product descriptions	For all levels of plan	Define the purpose and appearance of the product, its users, level of quality required, creation and checking skills.
4. Draw the product flow diagram	For all levels of plan	Define the sequence in which the products will be developed and any dependencies between them.

Quality review

A quality review is a structured assessment of a document conducted by a group of peers in a planned, documented and organised fashion. Its objectives are to:

- Assess the conformity of the document to set criteria;
- Involve key interested parties in checking the document's quality and thus promoting wider acceptance of the product;
- Provide confirmation that the product is complete and can be approved; and

- Advise that the product can be baselined for change control purposes.

There are four roles:

Table 36: Four Roles of Quality Review

Role	Description
1. Chair	• Control of preparation, review and follow-up • Sets agenda • Ensures focus
2. Presenter	• Represents the resource(s) that created the product • Answers questions
3. Reviewer	• Reviews product during preparation • Completes question list • Annotates the product with any spelling or grammatical errors • Gets answers during review • Chooses which follow-up actions to check
4. Administrator	• Organises location • Sends out invitations

	• Creates follow-up action list of any changes needed • Directed by chair

There are four steps:

Table 37: Four Steps of Quality Review

Step	Activity
1. Planning	• Date and attendees planned when creating stage and team plans
2. Preparation	• Location and duration • Invitations • Reviewers create question lists and submit to chair • Product annotated with any spelling or grammatical concerns • Chair creates agenda from question lists in consultation with presenter
3. Review	• Led by chair • Presenter answers reviewer questions • Administrator notes any changes on follow-up action list

	• Chair identifies who will action and who will check
4. Follow-up	• Changes made • Checked by reviewers • Progress chased by administrator • Chair confirms result to project manager

CHAPTER 4: TAILORING

PRINCE2® can be used on any type or size of project. It is designed to be tailored for each project. Tailoring means using the correct amount of planning and control, and the appropriate level of the processes and themes for a specific project.

The PRINCE2 principles are universal and will always apply. By comparing each principle to the project, the practitioner will understand how to adapt the theme to the project without losing its value.

Existing terms, procedures and forms

There is no problem in changing PRINCE2 terminology for terms long established in an organisation's projects. There is no problem in replacing suggested PRINCE2 forms with existing equivalents. And there is no problem in replacing procedures such as risk or change with tried-and-tested procedures already embedded in an organisation's culture.

Business case

All projects should have justification. Small projects may not need all the elements shown in the PRINCE2 business case product description, but there should always be reasons and a verifiable set of benefits or savings. If you judge that a business case is not needed, do you really have a project or is it just a work package?

Organisation

Roles can be shared or combined. However, PRINCE2 does not recommend sharing the executive or project manager role.

In a small project the project board may be one person, depending on who is supplying the development resources. The project manager may absorb the team manager role. Project support may be done by the project manager or part-time by a member of the development team. The project board may do its own project assurance.

In a large project there may need to be more than one senior user in order to fully represent the user needs. You may need more than one senior supplier in order to get supplier commitments. Remember that an alternative to having several senior suppliers could be to make the company's purchasing manager the senior supplier. Be wary of having too many senior users. Don't let them overwhelm the project board. If there are genuinely lots of them, put them in a user group with one spokesperson on the project board.

Remember that roles can be changed for different stages. If you no longer need a particular supplier for the next stage, remove that representative from the senior supplier role. Similarly, the skills you need for project assurance may well change from stage to stage, so don't be afraid to ring the changes.

Plans

In a small project you may not need teams, so no team plans. If you have only one development stage, can the detail necessary for day-to-day control be incorporated into the project plan?

Quality

For any project you need to know the quality aim and how you will meet that, so you will need the customer's quality expectations and acceptance criteria. Depending on the size of the project, you can then decide if quality needs can be taken care of by writing good product descriptions or whether you need to examine your quality management approach for other ways of checking quality. Remember to include the end user in your quality checking.

Risk

Every project should consider its risks. In a small project you may not need a full-blown risk management approach, but you must review risks before starting. The suggested problem register gives a good indication of what to consider.

Change

Even the smallest project should be ready for changes or additions. Just having the discipline to record these in the problem register should help you keep them under control.

You will need to decide how to identify project products and what form of version control is to be used. Once a product reaches a settled form, you should keep it somewhere 'safe' from uncontrolled change.

Progress

Ask yourself who the stakeholders are, even for small projects. Knowing what information to provide, when and how, should be enough, rather than writing a full communication management approach.

Documents

Not all documents or reports need to be formally written. Emails, telephone calls or word of mouth may be enough. Tailor product descriptions to local standards and project needs.

Processes

Processes can be combined or adapted, e.g. combining the SU and IP processes, combining CS and MP in small projects that do not use team managers.

GLOSSARY OF TERMS

Abbreviation	Definition
BAU	Business as usual
CIR	Configuration item record
CP	Closing a project (process)
CS	Controlling a stage (process)
DP	Directing a project (process)
IP	Initiating a project (process)
ISO	International standards Organisation
MoSCoW	Must have, should have, could have or won't have

MP	Managing product delivery (process)
O-S	Off-specification
PB	Project board
PBP	Product-based planning
PID	Project initiation documentation
PM	Project manager
PMT	Project management team
PRINCE2	Projects in a controlled environment
RFC	Request for change
Risk MS	Risk management strategy
SB	Managing a stage boundary (process)
SU	Senior user (project board role)

FURTHER READING

IT Governance Publishing (ITGP) is the world's leading publisher for governance and compliance. Our industry-leading pocket guides, books, training resources and toolkits are written by real-world practitioners and thought leaders. They are used globally by audiences of all levels, from students to C-suite executives.

Our high-quality publications cover all IT governance, risk and compliance frameworks and are available in a range of formats. This ensures our customers can access the information they need in the way they need it.

Our other publications about PRINCE2® include:

- *PRINCE2 Agile™ An Implementation Pocket Guide – Step-by-step advice for every project type* www.itgovernancepublishing.co.uk/product/prince2-agile-an-implementation-pocket-guide
- *PRINCE2® in Action – Project management in real terms* www.itgovernancepublishing.co.uk/product/prince2-in-action

For more information on ITGP and branded publishing services, and to view our full list of publications, visit www.itgovernancepublishing.co.uk.

To receive regular updates from ITGP, including information on new publications in your area(s) of interest, sign up for our newsletter at www.itgovernancepublishing.co.uk/topic/newsletter.

Branded publishing

Through our branded publishing service, you can customise ITGP publications with your company's branding.

Find out more at

www.itgovernancepublishing.co.uk/topic/branded-publishing-services.

Related services

ITGP is part of GRC International Group, which offers a comprehensive range of complementary products and services to help organisations meet their objectives.

For a full range of resources on PRINCE2 visit *www.itgovernance.co.uk/shop/category/prince2*.

Training services

The IT Governance training programme is built on our extensive practical experience designing and implementing management systems based on ISO standards, best practice and regulations.

Our courses help attendees develop practical skills and comply with contractual and regulatory requirements. They also support career development via recognised qualifications.

Learn more about our training courses in PRINCE2 and view the full course catalogue at *www.itgovernance.co.uk/training*.

Professional services and consultancy

We are a leading global consultancy of IT governance, risk management and compliance solutions. We advise businesses around the world on their most critical issues and present cost-saving and risk-reducing solutions based on international best practice and frameworks.

We offer a wide range of delivery methods to suit all budgets, timescales and preferred project approaches.

Find out how our consultancy services can help your organisation at *www.itgovernance.co.uk/consulting*.

Industry news

Want to stay up to date with the latest developments and resources in the IT governance and compliance market? Subscribe to our Daily Sentinel newsletter and we will send you mobile-friendly emails with fresh news and features about your preferred areas of interest, as well as unmissable offers and free resources to help you successfully start your projects. *www.itgovernance.co.uk/daily-sentinel*.

EU for product safety is Stephen Evans, The Mill Enterprise Hub, Stagreenan, Drogheda, Co. Louth, A92 CD3D, Ireland. (servicecentre@itgovernance.eu)

www.ingramcontent.com/pod-product-compliance
Lightning Source LLC
Chambersburg PA
CBHW070847070326
40690CB00009B/1729